WHEN GOD SEEMS SILENT: LESSONS FROM JOB

W. A. ALMILLA

Printed in the United States of America

ISBN: 9798309246632

Copyright © 2025 by W. A. Almilla

All rights reserved.

This book is a work of nonfiction, inspired by biblical accounts and personal reflections on the life of Job. While every effort has been made to ensure accuracy, the author make no representations or warranties regarding the completeness or applicability of the contents. Readers are encouraged to study the Scriptures for deeper insight.

Scripture quotations are taken from The Holy Bible, New International Version®, NIV®, copyright © 1973, 1978, 1984, 2011 by Biblica, Inc®. Used by permission. All rights reserved worldwide.

Scripture quotations marked NLT are taken from the Holy Bible, New Living Translation, copyright © 1996, 2004, 2015 by Tyndale House Foundation. Used by permission of Tyndale House Publishers, Carol Stream, Illinois 60188. All rights reserved.

For permission, inquiries, or to contact the author:

wilamy6265@gmail.com

Dedication

To all those who have walked through the valley of suffering, questioning, yet holding on to their faith—this book is for you.

As an evangelist of the Gospel of Christ, I have witnessed the pain of many faithful believers—men and women devoted to God, yet enduring trials that seem beyond understanding. Their silent tears, unspoken prayers, and unwavering trust in God, even when answers never came, have inspired me to write this book.

To the grieving hearts, the weary souls, and the faithful who find themselves in the silence of God—may Job's story bring you comfort and renewed strength. May you find peace in knowing that even in silence, God is working, refining, and preparing you for a greater purpose.

May His name be glorified through this work.

In Christ's love,
W. A. Almilla

TABLE OF CONTENTS

Dedication	3
Introduction	6
CHAPTER 1 - When The Righteous Suffer	8
CHAPTER 2 - The Weight of Suffering	14
CHAPTER 3 - Faulty Wisdom	21
CHAPTER 4 - Defending My Innocence	27
CHAPTER 5 - The Weight of False Accusations	35
CHAPTER 6 - My Redeemer Lives	42
CHAPTER 7 - Distorted Justice	50
CHAPTER 8 - From Honor to Despair	57
CHAPTER 9 - A Life Examined	65
CHAPTER 10 - Elihu Speaks	72
CHAPTER 11 - God's Justice and Power	78
CHAPTER 12 - Where Were You?	85
CHAPTER 13 - God's Ultimate Authority and Job's Restoration	91
CHAPTER 14 – Lessons From Job's Story	99
Acknowledgments	105
About the Author	107

Job 19:25

"I know that my Redeemer lives, and that in the end he will stand on the earth."

Introduction

The Book of Job is one of the most profound and thought-provoking books in the Bible. It explores the age-old question: Why do the righteous suffer? Set in an ancient time before Israel's covenant laws, Job's story delves into the complexities of human suffering, divine justice, and faith.

Job, a wealthy and upright man, becomes the subject of a heavenly test when Satan challenges his righteousness, arguing that he serves God only because of his blessings. With God's permission, Job endures unimaginable loss—his wealth, health, and family are taken from him. As he sits in agony and despair, his three friends—Eliphaz, Bildad, and Zophar—arrive, attempting to explain his suffering through traditional wisdom: God blesses the righteous and punishes the wicked. However, their arguments fail to comfort Job, who maintains his innocence and questions God's justice.

A young man, Elihu, eventually speaks, offering a different perspective—suggesting that suffering serves as divine instruction rather than punishment. Finally, God Himself responds, not by explaining Job's suffering but by revealing His sovereignty over creation. Job humbly repents, acknowledging God's wisdom beyond human understanding.

In the end, God restores Job's fortunes, demonstrating that faithfulness is not in vain. The Book of Job reminds readers that suffering is not always a sign of God's displeasure, but an opportunity to trust Him, even in the unknown.

As you journey through this book, may you find encouragement and strength, knowing that even when God seems silent, He is never absent.

CHAPTER 1 - When The Righteous Suffer

A Test of Faith and Friends

Job Chapter 1 to Job Chapter 4

Job's story opens with a scene on earth where he serves as a priest for his household, offering sacrifices much like Abel and Noah did. He recognizes that the shedding of an animal's blood can serve as a means of purification for his children—foreshadowing the sacrificial system later established in Israel. Meanwhile, in the heavenly realm, God commends Job's righteousness, but Satan questions his sincerity, suggesting that Job's faithfulness is driven by personal gain. To test this, God permits Satan to strip Job of his possessions and afflict his body. Despite his suffering, Job remains steadfast in his reverence for God. Three friends arrive to console him, initially sitting in silence, following ancient customs. However, as they begin to speak, a lengthy dialogue unfolds, exploring the age-old question of why the righteous suffer. Overcome with anguish, Job laments the day of his birth.

Divine Testimony About Job

In **Job 1:8**, God Himself gives a remarkable testimony about Job's character:

> *"Have you considered my servant Job? There is no one on earth like him; he is blameless and upright, a man who fears God and shuns evil." - Job 1:8*

This divine statement highlights Job's exceptional righteousness, integrity, and reverence for God. Job is not sinless, but he lives a life devoted to God, avoiding evil and seeking righteousness. God's testimony about Job establishes him as an example of faithfulness, making his suffering even more striking since he did not bring it upon himself through sin.

Job Understand Sacrifices, And In The Biblical Story, Other People Offered Sacrifices.

Job offers sacrifices as an act of worship and intercession. In **Job 1:5**, he sacrifices burnt offerings for each of his children, saying:

> *"Perhaps my children have sinned and cursed God in their hearts."*

This shows that Job understands sacrifices as a means of atonement, even for sins that might have been committed unknowingly. His practice reflects a deep sense of spiritual responsibility and reverence for God.

Throughout the Bible, sacrifices are a key component of worship:

- **Genesis 4:3-5** – Cain and Abel offer sacrifices, with Abel's offering being accepted by God.
- **Genesis 8:20-21** – Noah offers a burnt offering after the flood, and God responds favorably.
- **Genesis 22:13** – Abraham is willing to sacrifice Isaac but God provides a ram as a substitute.
- **Exodus and Leviticus** – The sacrificial system is formally instituted under the Law of Moses for the atonement of sins.

Job's sacrificial practice predates the Mosaic Law, indicating an early understanding of substitutionary atonement, where an offering is made to seek God's favor and forgiveness.

What does the text teach us about Job's accuser? Is he a member of "the heavenly court," and how does God limit what he can do?

In **Job 1:6-7**, Satan appears among "the sons of God" before the Lord. This suggests that he has access to the heavenly court, though he does not belong to it in the same way as the angels who serve God.

Satan, whose name means "accuser" or "adversary," challenges Job's righteousness, arguing that Job is faithful only because of his prosperity. He accuses God of being unjust by implying that people serve Him only for rewards, not out of genuine devotion.

God permits Satan to test Job but sets strict limits:

- **First limitation** (Job 1:12): Satan may take away Job's possessions but must not harm him physically.
- **Second limitation** (Job 2:6): Satan may afflict Job's body but must not take his life.

This teaches us that Satan operates only within the boundaries God allows. He does not have absolute power but is subject to divine authority.

Job respond to Satan's attacks, and what does his response teach all believers about responding to the enemy?

Job's response is one of humility, worship, and faith:

1. **After losing his wealth and children**, Job **worships** God instead of cursing Him:
   "Naked I came from my mother's womb, and naked I will depart. The Lord gave and the Lord has taken away; may the name of the Lord be praised." - Job 1:21

2. **After being afflicted with painful sores**, Job **refuses to curse God**:
   "Shall we accept good from God, and not trouble?" - Job 2:10

3. **In Job 3**, he finally expresses his grief but does not sin against God. Instead, he laments his suffering, showing that deep sorrow and faith can coexist.

Lessons for Believers in Responding to the Enemy

1. **Worship in the midst of trials** – Job praised God despite his suffering, teaching believers to remain

faithful even when they don't understand God's ways.

2. **Recognize God's sovereignty** – Job acknowledged that everything he had came from God and that God's purposes are beyond human understanding.

3. **Do not curse God in suffering** – Even when encouraged to do so by his wife, Job refused to turn against God.

4. **Be honest with God about struggles** – Job's lament in chapter 3 shows that expressing pain is not sinful. Faith does not mean suppressing emotions, but bringing them before God.

Ultimately, Job's response demonstrates that **true faith is not dependent on circumstances but on trust in God's character**. His story challenges believers to stand firm in trials, knowing that even when God seems silent, He is always in control.

CHAPTER 2 - The Weight of Suffering

Job's Cry for Justice and Comfort

Job Chapter 5 to Chapter 7

Eliphaz adheres to a belief in "justice theology," where individuals receive what they deserve. He encourages Job to bring his case before God, believing that divine discipline and correction would follow. Job, on the other hand, insists on his right to lament and maintains his innocence. Their perspectives reflect common human tendencies—like Eliphaz, people often demand justice for others while hoping for grace themselves. Observers of suffering frequently search for reasons behind it. Meanwhile, like Job, those enduring hardship tend to question their circumstances, assume their own innocence, and long for immediate relief. Both men grapple with suffering from their respective viewpoints, yet neither fully understands God's purpose in Job's trials. Unaware of the heavenly dialogue, Eliphaz resorts to judgment while Job responds with complaint.

Eliphaz believe that suffering is a discipline from God.

Eliphaz sees human suffering as a form of divine discipline or correction from God. He argues that trouble is inevitable in life:

> *"Yet man is born to trouble as surely as sparks fly upward." - Job 5:7*

His counsel to Job is to **accept suffering as God's discipline** and seek God's favor:

> *"Blessed is the one whom God corrects; so do not despise the discipline of the Almighty." - Job 5:17*

Eliphaz believes that if Job humbles himself and turns to God, his fortunes will be restored (Job 5:18-27). His advice is well-intended but flawed because he assumes that all suffering is a result of God's correction rather than considering other reasons for Job's affliction.

Eliphaz Believe That Job Is Being Disciplined

Eliphaz operates under the assumption that **suffering is always caused by sin** and that Job must have done something wrong to deserve his misfortune. He believes that Job's affliction is God's way of correcting him:

> *"For hardship does not spring from the soil, nor does trouble sprout from the ground." - Job 5:6*

This means Eliphaz sees suffering as a consequence of human actions—implying that Job is being punished or disciplined for hidden sins. However, Eliphaz does not have knowledge of the divine conversation between God and Satan (Job 1-2), where it was revealed that Job's suffering was a test of faith, not a punishment for wrongdoing.

Eliphaz Attitude Teach Us About How We View The Suffering Of Others

Eliphaz's response teaches an important lesson: **we must be careful not to assume that suffering is always the result of sin or divine punishment**. His rigid theology fails to consider other reasons why people suffer, such as spiritual testing, refinement of character, or the mystery of God's purposes.

His attitude reflects the danger of **misjudging others' pain** and offering **insensitive counsel** instead of true compassion. When people suffer, they need understanding, not accusations. Job's experience warns us against assuming we fully understand God's reasons for someone's suffering.

Job Believe He Has The Right To Complain

Job believes he has a right to complain because his suffering is unbearable and beyond human endurance. He compares his pain to **"arrows of the Almighty"** and describes himself as longing for death:

> *"Oh, that I might have my request, that God would grant what I hope for, that God would be willing to crush me, to let loose his hand and cut off my life!" - Job 6:8-9*

Unlike Eliphaz, who sees suffering as a form of discipline, Job views it as **an overwhelming burden that makes no sense**. He believes that his affliction is unfair and questions why God allows it to continue.

This teaches us that it is not wrong to **express our pain and ask hard questions** before God. Job's honesty shows that true faith does not mean suppressing emotions but bringing them before the Lord.

Job Was Feeling Hopeless

Job's hope is **crushed under the weight of his suffering**. He sees no reason to continue living and **feels abandoned by God**:

> "What strength do I have, that I should still hope? What prospects, that I should be patient?" - Job 6:11

His despair reflects how intense suffering can shake a person's faith and make them feel utterly hopeless. However, despite his anguish, Job does not turn away from God—he simply longs for an answer.

This teaches us that even the strongest believers can struggle with hopelessness, but God remains sovereign even in those moments.

Job Was Disappointed Of His Friends In Their Assumptions About Him

Job is deeply disappointed by his friends' counsel. He describes their words as unreliable and compares them to a dry stream that deceives travelers expecting water:

> *"Now you too have proved to be of no help; you see something dreadful and are afraid." - Job 6:21*

His friends assume that Job has sinned and brought this suffering upon himself. They fail to understand that Job is innocent and that his suffering is part of a greater spiritual battle.

Conclusion

In these chapters, we see two contrasting views on suffering:

1. **Eliphaz believes suffering is divine discipline** and assumes Job is guilty.
2. **Job believes his suffering is unjust** and struggles to understand why God allows it.

This section of Job challenges us to think deeply about how we respond to suffering—both in our own lives and in the lives of others. It teaches us that **not all suffering is punishment**, that we must be careful in how we counsel the afflicted, and that God invites us to bring our honest emotions before Him.

CHAPTER 3 - Faulty Wisdom

When Friends Misjudge and God's Ways Remain Unseen

Job Chapter 8 to Chapter 11

Bildad interprets suffering as the consequence of wickedness, assuming that Job's children must have sinned or that Job himself has strayed from God. He advises Job to seek God earnestly and live righteously, believing that such actions will lead to restoration and a return to prosperity (Job 8:6). However, his overly simplistic reasoning offers no comfort to Job, whose life has been completely upended. Job, unable to sense God's presence, longs for a mediator.

Zophar joins the discussion, urging Job to stop speaking foolishly. Like Bildad, he insists that Job's suffering would end if he simply repented of his sins. However, suffering is not always a direct result of personal wrongdoing; atonement through sacrifice addresses sin. Job, overwhelmed with confusion, doubt, and despair, continues to insist on his innocence. What he does not yet realize is that his righteousness depends on God's approval, and divine favor does not necessarily guarantee a life free from suffering.

What is the source of Bildad's authority?

Bildad draws his authority from **tradition and the wisdom of the past generations**. Unlike Eliphaz, who claimed to have received wisdom through visions (Job 4:12-17), Bildad argues that truth comes from history:

> *"Ask the former generations and find out what their ancestors learned." - Job 8:8*

He believes that the experiences and teachings of the past provide a clear understanding of how God deals with people. His approach is rooted in the idea that the righteous are always blessed and the wicked always suffer, which leads him to assume that Job must have done something wrong.

Insensitive Speech Of Bildad Adding To Job's Distress

Bildad assumes that **Job's children must have died because of their sin** and that Job is also suffering due to some wrongdoing:

> *"When your children sinned against him, he gave them over to the penalty of their sin." - Job 8:4*

This assumption makes Bildad's speech **harsh and insensitive**. Instead of offering comfort, he argues that if Job were truly innocent, God would already have restored him:

> *"If you are pure and upright, even now he will rouse himself on your behalf and restore you to your prosperous state." - Job 8:6*

His rigid theology fails to consider any other reason for suffering apart from punishment for sin. This leads him to **wrongly accuse Job**, adding to his distress instead of helping him find peace.

Job Understanding About God Shapes His Thinking And Guides His Responses

Job understands that **God's wisdom and power are far beyond human comprehension**. He acknowledges that no one can argue with God's sovereign decisions:

"How then can I dispute with him? How can I find words to argue with him?" - Job 9:14

Job realizes that **God is just but also mysterious**—His ways are not always predictable. Unlike his friends, who believe that suffering must always be the result of sin, Job recognizes that God's purposes might be beyond human understanding:

"He performs wonders that cannot be fathomed, miracles that cannot be counted." - Job 9:10

This understanding shape Job's responses, as he refuses to falsely confess sins he did not commit just to satisfy his friends' accusations. Instead, he longs for clarity from God.

Job asks for mediator to help him bring his arguments to God.

Job asks for a **mediator**—someone who could stand between him and God to present his case:

> *"If only there were someone to mediate between us, someone to bring us together."* - *Job 9:33*

Job feels that as a mere human, he **cannot contend with God's greatness**. He recognizes his limitations and desires someone who could bridge the gap between himself and the Almighty.

This request highlights Job's deep longing for justice and understanding. He believes that such a mediator would be necessary because:

1. **God is too great and powerful** – Job feels unworthy to plead his case directly before Him.
2. **Job sees himself as helpless** – He knows he cannot "win" an argument with God but wants to be heard.
3. **He believes God is just, but he doesn't understand His actions** – Job desires an explanation, but he also

knows that human reasoning is inadequate compared to God's wisdom.

Conclusion

In Job 8 to 11, we see a contrast between Bildad's rigid belief that suffering is always due to sin and Job's deeper understanding that God's ways are beyond human logic. While Job's friends wrongly accuse him, Job acknowledges God's power, questions his suffering, and longs for a mediator—a role that ultimately points to Jesus Christ, who later becomes the ultimate intercessor between God and humanity.

These chapters remind us that in times of suffering, human wisdom is often flawed, but God's wisdom is perfect, even when it is beyond our understanding.

CHAPTER 4 - Defending My Innocence

Job's Struggle with Divine Justice

Job Chapter 12 to Chapter 14

The escalating tension in the conversations, combined with Job's deteriorating health, leads to his harsh response, where he labels his friends as arrogant, deceitful, and mocking. Frustrated, he urges them to remain silent. Job also directs his anguish toward God, blaming Him for his suffering and pleading for an explanation of any wrongdoing. Once again, he wishes for death as an escape from his pain.

Job openly expresses the thoughts that many who suffer hesitate to voice. People often speak candidly about their struggles with those they can see—if they could visibly encounter God, they might address Him just as honestly. Through his words to both God and his friends, Job wrestles with his emotions, attempting to make sense of his pain. The book of Job provides a space for sufferers to process their thoughts, confront their fears, and express deep sorrow.

Job's raw and honest words resonate with all who endure suffering.

What does Job imply when he accuses his friends of dishonestly defending God?

Job rebukes his friends for speaking **falsehoods in their attempt to defend God**. He accuses them of misrepresenting God's justice by assuming that **all suffering is punishment for sin**:

"Will you speak wickedly on God's behalf? Will you speak deceitfully for him?" - Job 13:7

Job is saying that his friends are twisting the truth to fit their **simplistic theology**—that only the wicked suffer and the righteous prosper. By insisting that Job must be guilty, they are misrepresenting God's wisdom and justice.

This is a warning against **misusing theology to explain suffering**. Sometimes, in trying to "defend" God, people end up distorting the truth and causing more harm than good.

What does Job say about their platitudes, and what platitudes do we sometimes try to offer others when they suffer?

Job criticizes his friends for offering **empty words and clichés** instead of true comfort:

> *"Your maxims are proverbs of ashes; your defenses are defenses of clay." - Job 13:12*

He sees their words as **worthless and fragile**, like ashes and crumbling clay. Their arguments do not truly address his pain; instead, they add to his suffering by falsely accusing him.

Common Platitudes We Offer in Suffering

Like Job's friends, people today often use **oversimplified phrases** when comforting those who suffer. Some examples include:

1. **"Everything happens for a reason."**
   - While true in a broad sense, it doesn't always comfort in the moment.
2. **"God won't give you more than you can handle."**

- This is a misunderstanding of Scripture—sometimes suffering is overwhelming, and we need God's strength.
3. **"Just have more faith, and things will get better."**
    - This can make someone feel guilty for struggling, rather than offering real comfort.

Job's frustration reminds us that when people are suffering, they need presence, understanding, and honesty, not shallow words.

Two Things Job Ask God To Do For Him So That He Can Face Him

Job asks God for two specific things before he is willing to approach Him:

1. **Remove His hand of suffering:**
"Only grant me these two things, God, and then I will not hide from you: Withdraw your hand far from me, and stop frightening me with your terrors." - Job 13:20-21

Job is overwhelmed by pain and feels like God's hand is too heavy upon him. He wants relief so he can speak openly.

2. **Give him an opportunity to speak without fear**
"Then summon me and I will answer, or let me speak, and you reply to me." - Job 13:22

Job desires a **fair hearing** before God. He wants to either answer God's charges against him or speak and receive a reply. He longs for clarity, justice, and a response from Almighty.

These requests show **Job's deep desire for a personal encounter with God**, rather than simply accepting his friends' flawed explanations.

Job Expressed His Hope About The Resurrection

Job wrestles with the finality of death, asking whether there is hope beyond the grave:

"But a man dies and is laid low; he breathes his last and is no more." - Job 14:10

At this moment, **Job struggles with doubt**—he does not have a clear revelation of resurrection as we see in the New Testament. However, he expresses a **hopeful longing**:

> *"If someone dies, will they live again? All the days of my hard service I will wait for my renewal to come."* - Job 14:14

He imagines a time when God **might call him back to life**:

> *"You will call and I will answer you; you will long for the creature your hands have made."* - Job 14:15

This suggests that **Job has an instinctive hope that God is not finished with humanity after death**, even though he does not yet fully grasp the resurrection as revealed later in Scripture.

Job Suffering Lead Him To Question God's Justice

Job's suffering leads him to lament the harshness of life and question God's justice:

1. He feels **forgotten and overwhelmed**: *"So you destroy a person's hope."* - Job 14:19

2. He **wonders if life is worth anything**: *"Man's days are determined; you have decreed the number of his months and have set limits he cannot exceed."* - Job 14:5

3. He **despairs at the fleeting nature of life**: *"Mortals, born of woman, are of few days and full of trouble."* - Job 14:1

Job's suffering **pushes him to deep sorrow, frustration, and even despair**, but he never completely abandons his faith. His honesty before God teaches us that faith does not mean suppressing pain—it means bringing it before the Lord with sincerity.

Conclusion

In **Job 12 to 14**, we see a man who is misunderstood by his friends, struggling to make sense of his suffering, and longing for a response from God. His words teach us valuable lessons:

1. We must be careful not to defend God with falsehoods or shallow words when comforting others.

2. God invites us to bring our honest emotions before Him—lament is not a lack of faith, but an expression of trust.
3. Even in deep suffering, Job clings to a faint hope that God is not done with him yet.

Though Job does not yet fully understand the resurrection, his words foreshadow the greater hope revealed in Jesus Christ—who would ultimately answer Job's longing for a mediator and the promise of life beyond the grave.

CHAPTER 5 - The Weight of False Accusations

Struggle Against Harsh Judgment

Job Chapter 15 to Chapter 18

Like many, Eliphaz struggles to handle raw emotion and honest discussion. He dismisses Job's passionate words as mere "empty chatter" (Job 15:3), attributing them to personal sin. Relying on his own experiences and the wisdom passed down by previous generations, Eliphaz upholds his belief that people receive what they deserve—insisting that those who live in fear do so rightfully. Job, in turn, responds sharply, asserting that if their roles were reversed, he would offer comfort rather than condemnation. Feeling abandoned by God, Job mistakenly assumes that God does not love him and once again appeals for a mediator (Job 16:21; see 9:33). No human fully comprehends God's plan, making it easy to misjudge Him. Suffering can cloud one's understanding of both God and oneself. While Job urges his friends to remain silent, he might have benefited from doing the same.

How does Eliphaz respond to Job's accusations against him and his friends?

Eliphaz responds to Job with **even harsher accusations** than before. Instead of offering comfort, he rebukes Job for his bold words against his friends and against God:

1. He accuses Job of **arrogance and empty talk**: *"Would a wise person answer with empty notions or fill their belly with the hot east wind?"* - Job 15:2
2. He claims that **Job's own words condemn him**: *"Your own mouth condemns you, not mine; your own lips testify against you."* - Job 15:6
3. He insists that **Job must be suffering because of sin** and warns that the wicked always face destruction.

Eliphaz refuses to believe that Job is innocent. Instead, he sees Job's suffering as proof that he has sinned, reinforcing his flawed belief that **God always punishes the wicked in this life and rewards the righteous**.

Eliphaz relies on tradition to understand God, though it can sometimes be an unreliable source of truth.

Eliphaz's arguments rely heavily on traditional wisdom passed down from past generations:

"I will tell you, hear me; what I have seen I will declare— what the wise have declared, hiding nothing received from their ancestors." - Job 15:17-18

His belief system is based on a rigid view of divine justice:

1. The righteous prosper.
2. The wicked suffer.
3. Therefore, Job must be wicked.

Why is tradition sometimes an unreliable guide for truth?

1. **Tradition is not always complete** – Eliphaz and his friends fail to see that **God's justice is not always immediate**; sometimes the righteous suffer for reasons beyond human understanding.
2. **Tradition can be based on human assumptions** – Just because something has been passed down does not mean it is always right. Eliphaz's reasoning

ignores the possibility that suffering can be a test, not a punishment.

3. **God's ways are beyond human traditions** – Job understands that God's justice is deeper than the simple formula of "good things happen to good people, bad things happen to bad people."

This teaches us that while tradition can offer **wisdom**, we must **always test it against the full truth of God's Word** and His revealed character.

How does Job characterize God in this section?

As Job struggles with his suffering and the harsh words of his friends, his view of God becomes more conflicted:

1. **God is powerful but seems to be against him**: *"God assails me and tears me in his anger and gnashes his teeth at me." - Job 16:9*
2. **He feels abandoned and betrayed**: *"God has turned me over to the ungodly and thrown me into the clutches of the wicked." - Job 16:11*
3. **But Job still believes in divine justice** and longs for a heavenly witness:

"Even now my witness is in heaven; my advocate is on high." - Job 16:19

Despite his deep despair, Job does not turn away from God completely. Instead, he **pleads for a mediator**—someone who will argue his case before God.

This longing foreshadows the role of **Jesus Christ**, who would later come as the ultimate mediator between God and humanity.

Job deal with the depth of his loss, the shame of his situation, and the accusations from his friends.

Job faces an overwhelming combination of grief, public shame, and false accusations, yet he responds in several ways:

- **He pours out his pain honestly before God** – He does not hold back his emotions but expresses his sorrow fully.
- **He continues to seek justice from God** – Even though he feels abandoned, he still looks to God for answers.

- **He rebukes his friends for their cruelty** – Job tells them that instead of comforting him, they have become his tormentors:

  "How long will you torment me and crush me with words?" - Job 19:2

Despite everything, Job clings to **a faint hope in God's justice**, showing that even in suffering, faith does not mean having all the answers—it means continuing to trust in God's ultimate righteousness.

Conclusion

In **Job 15-18**, we see the intense struggle between human understanding and divine mystery:

1. **Eliphaz and Bildad rely on flawed tradition**, assuming Job's suffering means he has sinned.
2. **Job wrestles with despair, yet still longs for a heavenly advocate** who will plead his case.
3. **His friends add to his suffering rather than offering true comfort**, reminding us to be compassionate in the face of others' pain.

Ultimately, these chapters remind us that **God's justice is greater than human wisdom**, and even in silence, He is still at work.

CHAPTER 6 - My Redeemer Lives

Holding on to Faith Amid Injustice

Job Chapter 19 to Chapter 21

In **Job 19**, Job expresses deep despair, feeling abandoned by both **his friends and God**. He pleads for compassion, lamenting that **his suffering has made him a stranger to everyone**. Yet, in a powerful declaration of faith, he proclaims, **"I know that my Redeemer lives"** - Job 19:25, expressing hope that one day, God will vindicate him.

Zophar responds in Job 20, arguing that the **wicked prosper only briefly** and will ultimately face **divine judgment**. He insists that **sin leads to ruin**, portraying a harsh view of **God's justice** that leaves no room for Job's innocence.

In **Job 21**, Job refutes Zophar, pointing out that **many wicked people live long, prosperous lives** without facing immediate judgment. He challenges the simplistic idea that suffering is always punishment for sin, emphasizing that

*God's justice does not always unfold in ways humans expect. Job remains **troubled and unanswered**.*

What charges does Job bring against God?

Job, in his deep suffering, feels that God has turned against him and become his enemy:

1. **God has wronged him**:
   "Though I cry, 'Violence!' I get no response; though I call for help, there is no justice." - Job 19:7

2. **God has stripped him of honor and left him abandoned**:
   "He has stripped me of my honor and removed the crown from my head." - Job 19:9

3. **God has blocked every path and torn down his hope**:
   "He has blocked my way so I cannot pass; he has shrouded my paths in darkness." - Job 19:8

4. **God has turned friends and family against him**:
   "My relatives have gone away; my closest friends have forgotten me." - Job 19:14

Have You Ever Accused God In Challenging Times?

Many believers experience moments when they **question God's justice** during suffering. Like Job, we may feel forgotten, abandoned, or that God is unfairly allowing pain in our lives. However, Job's story teaches us that even when we bring accusations against God, He **does not reject honest struggles**—instead, He invites us to bring our pain before Him.

Job Request From His Friends

Job pleads for mercy and understanding from his friends instead of their harsh judgments:

> *"Have pity on me, my friends, have pity, for the hand of God has struck me." - Job 19:21*

He begs them to stop attacking him and falsely assuming that he has sinned. Instead of offering comfort, they have made his suffering worse by acting as judges rather than as friends.

This teaches us an important lesson: when people are suffering, they need compassion, not accusations.

Job express hope in this passage, Job 19:25-27. Despite his deep suffering, Job declares one of the most powerful statements of faith in the entire book:

"I know that my redeemer lives, and that in the end he will stand on the earth." - Job 19:25

He believes that:

- **A Redeemer (or Vindicator) will come** – Someone will plead his case and restore justice.
- **Even after death, he will see God** – He holds on to hope that, somehow, he will be restored in God's presence.

This is one of the earliest glimpses of resurrection hope in the Bible, pointing forward to Jesus Christ as the ultimate Redeemer.

How do his words here compare with his perspective on the afterlife in Job 14:10-15?

In **Job 14:10-15**, Job was **uncertain and doubtful** about what happens after death:

"But a man dies and is laid low; he breathes his last and is no more." - Job 14:10

He **wonders if there is life after death** but does not express certainty. However, by **Job 19:25-27**, he has moved from uncertainty to **a bold declaration of faith**—that he will see God even after his flesh is destroyed.

This shows that even in suffering, faith can grow and deepen over time.

Zophar and Job differ in their views of God's response to wickedness.

Zophar and Job have **opposing views** on how God deals with the wicked:

- **Zophar (Job 20)** argues that the wicked always face swift judgment:
    - *"The triumph of the wicked has been short-lived."* - Job 20:5
    - He believes that sinners **never truly prosper** and that God will bring immediate justice in their lifetime.

- **Job (Job 21)**, on the other hand, observes that the wicked often **prosper in this life**:
  - *"Why do the wicked live on, growing old and increasing in power?" - Job 21:7*
  - Job challenges the assumption that **only the righteous prosper**, noting that many wicked people die in peace, rich and satisfied.

This reveals a profound theological truth: **God's justice is not always immediate**. While Zophar sees justice as quick and predictable, Job recognizes that **God's ways are not always understood in this life**.

How do you respond when you see the wicked experience success?

Many believers wrestle with the same question as Job—why do evil people seem to prosper while the righteous suffer? Psalm 73 echoes this struggle:

"For I envied the arrogant when I saw the prosperity of the wicked." - Psalm 73:3

However, both Job and Psalm 73 remind us that:

1. **God's justice is not always immediate** – The wicked may prosper temporarily, but ultimate justice belongs to God.
2. **We must focus on eternal perspective** – True reward and judgment come not in this short life, but in eternity.
3. **Trusting in God's sovereignty brings peace** – Even when things seem unfair, we are called to trust in God's greater plan.

Conclusion

In **Job 19-21**, Job moves from despair to **one of the most powerful declarations of faith in the Bible.** Even as his friends misjudge him, he clings to the truth that **his Redeemer lives** and that he will see God.

1. **His friends insist that suffering means guilt**, but Job holds on to the mystery of God's justice.
2. **Zophar believes the wicked are always punished immediately**, while Job observes that sometimes they prosper.

3. **Through his suffering, Job begins to see beyond this life and into eternity**, foreshadowing the hope of Christ's redemption.

These chapters remind us that even when life seems unfair, God is still in control, and ultimate justice belongs to Him.

CHAPTER 7 - Distorted Justice

Accusations, Despair, and the Greatness of God

Job Chapter 22 to Chapter 25

Eliphaz's words expose his flawed understanding of suffering. He firmly believes that the righteous do not suffer, leading him to conclude that Job must be unrighteous. He assumes that Job's suffering is a direct result of his failure to do good for others and urges him to change his ways to find peace. However, when Job examines himself, he sees innocence where his friends see guilt. His frustration grows as their accusations multiply, while God remains silent. Job observes that the wicked seem to prosper, enjoying blessings while he appears cursed. Bildad asserts that no one is truly innocent before God. Ultimately, the conversation between Job and his friends offers no real help—Job speaks from pain, while his friends rely on tradition and personal experience. Each of them speaks only partial truths, as they lack the full revelation of God.

What specific sins does Eliphaz accuse Job of, and what does he advise Job to do to restore his relationship with God?

Eliphaz **falsely accuses Job** of serious sins, assuming that Job's suffering must be a result of his wickedness. He charges Job with:

1. **Exploiting the poor** – *"You must have lent money to your friend and demanded clothing as security. Yes, you stripped him to the bone!" - Job 22:6, NLT*
2. **Neglecting widows and orphans** – *"You must have refused water for the thirsty and food for the hungry." - Job 22:7, NLT*
3. **Taking advantage of the needy** – *"You must have sent widows away empty-handed and crushed the hopes of orphans." - Job 22:9, NLT*

Eliphaz's Solution:

He urges Job to repent and submit to God, promising that God will restore him:

"Submit to God, and you will have peace; then things will go well for you." - Job 22:21, NLT

Eliphaz assumes that Job's suffering is because of sin and that if he simply turns back to God, everything will be fixed. However, Eliphaz is wrong—Job is innocent, and his suffering is not due to wickedness but a divine test beyond human understanding.

Job's response reflect everyone's experience when accused of things they know are not true.

Job's response reflects the frustration, pain, and isolation that many people feel when falsely accused:

1. **He longs for a chance to defend himself before God** –
   "If only I knew where to find God, I would go to his court." - Job 23:3, NLT
   → Like Job, people who are wrongly accused desire justice and vindication.
2. **He maintains his innocence but feels unheard** –
   "I have not departed from his commands, but have treasured his words more than daily food." - Job

23:12, NLT

→ This shows the emotional toll of being misunderstood, even when one has done nothing wrong.

3. **He feels that God is distant** –

"I go east, but he is not there. I go west, but I cannot find him." - Job 23:8, NLT

→ Many believers experience this when facing unjust suffering, feeling abandoned despite their faithfulness.

Despite all this, Job does not abandon his faith—he trusts that God knows the truth, even when others do not. Job describes his present experience, and said something will happen when this experience ends.

Job describes his present experience as one of intense fear, suffering, and uncertainty:

1. **He feels overwhelmed by darkness** – *"God has made my heart faint; the Almighty has terrified me." - Job 23:16, NLT*

2. **He sees injustice everywhere** – *"Why doesn't the Almighty bring the wicked to judgment?" - Job 24:1, NLT*

What Job Believes Will Happen Eventually:

God knows his path and will bring him through the trial purified –

> *"When he has tested me, I will come out as pure as gold." - Job 23:10, NLT*

> → This shows **Job's unshaken faith** that despite everything, God's justice will prevail.

This reflects the experience of many believers—suffering feels endless, but God's refining process brings spiritual growth.

What specific sins does Job say the wicked keep on doing, and what does he say God will do in the end?

Job lists the evil actions of the wicked, showing that their sin is real and ongoing:

1. **Stealing land and property** – *"The wicked remove landmarks; they steal livestock and put them in their own pastures." - Job 24:2, NLT*
2. **Oppressing the poor and needy** – *"They force the poor to go without clothing; they take the sheaves of grain from the hungry." - Job 24:10, NLT*
3. **Murdering and preying on the helpless** – *"The murderer rises in the early dawn to kill the poor and needy; at night he is a thief." - Job 24:14, NLT*

Job's Perspective on God's Judgment:

1. He **wonders why God does not immediately punish the wicked**:
   "The wicked go to bed rich but wake to find that all their wealth is gone." - Job 24:24, NLT
2. He **believes that ultimately, God will bring justice**:

   "Their candles are snuffed out in the darkness. Their branches will be broken." - Job 24:20, NLT

This struggle—**why does God allow the wicked to prosper?**—is a major theme throughout Scripture (see Psalm 73). Job doesn't yet have a full answer, but he holds on to the truth that **God will eventually judge the wicked** in His time.

Conclusion

1. Eliphaz wrongly accuses Job of sin, urging him to repent to be restored.
2. Job deeply struggles with false accusations, longing to plead his case before God.
3. Job describes his suffering as overwhelming, but he believes God will refine him like gold.
4. Job acknowledges that the wicked seem to prosper, but he holds onto the truth that God will ultimately bring justice.

This passage teaches us to trust in God's justice even when life seems unfair and to remain faithful, knowing that suffering is often a refining process that strengthens our faith.

CHAPTER 8 - From Honor to Despair

God's Power, Wisdom, and Lost Blessings

Job Chapter 26 to Chapter 29

Job and his friends hold theological beliefs that shape their understanding of life's challenges. However, Job's theology crumbles under the immense weight of his suffering. Instead of providing comfort, his friends' responses only intensify his emotional and physical distress, leaving him defensive, bitter, and despondent. In his search for meaning, Job contemplates the nature of wisdom and ultimately concludes that true wisdom comes from God alone. Reflecting on his past blessings, he recalls the deep sense of God's friendship and the honor he once enjoyed, as both the young and old respected him. He had been a source of help for the marginalized—the poor, the blind, the lame, orphans, widows, and strangers—using his influence to stand against oppression. Life had been good for everyone connected to him. But his suffering changed everything, and those who once benefited from his generosity also felt the effects of his downfall. Job's experience highlights how one person's suffering can ripple outward, impacting many lives.

In what ways does Job's depiction of creation in Job 26:7-14 reflect the creation narrative in Genesis?

In **Job 26:7-14**, Job describes God's power in creation, which closely mirrors the Genesis account:

1. **God hangs the earth on nothing** – *"God stretches the northern sky over empty space and hangs the earth on nothing." - Job 26:7, NLT*
   - This aligns with **Genesis 1:1**, where God creates the heavens and the earth from nothing.
2. **He controls the waters and boundaries** – *"He wraps the rain in his thick clouds, and the clouds don't burst with the weight." - Job 26:8, NLT*
   - Similar to **Genesis 1:6-7**, where God separates the waters above and below.
3. **God marks the horizon and brings light** – *"He created the horizon when he separated the waters; he set the boundary between day and night." - Job 26:10, NLT*

- This reflects **Genesis 1:4-5**, when God separates light from darkness.

Both Job and Genesis **emphasize God's sovereign power in creation**, showing that the world was not formed by chance but by divine design.

Job calls the wonders of creation a "whisper of his power" (Job 26:14), what does this say about God?

Job marvels at the vastness of God's power, yet he recognizes that everything humans see is only a small glimpse of God's full majesty:

"These are just the beginning of all that he does, merely a whisper of his power. Who, then, can comprehend the thunder of his power?" - Job 26:14, NLT

This means that:

1. **God's power is beyond human understanding** – Even the wonders of creation are just a "whisper" compared to His true greatness.
2. **If creation is so grand, how much greater is God Himself?** – If the universe is vast and complex, how much more powerful is the One who created it?

3. **It points to God's sovereignty** – Job understands that God is not limited by human comprehension or circumstances.

This verse reminds us that what we know about God **is only a fraction** of His full glory, and we must trust in His greatness even when we don't understand His ways.

Job Determined To Defend His Integrity

1. **He knows he is innocent** – He refuses to falsely confess sins he did not commit:
   "I will never concede that you are right; I will defend my integrity until I die." - Job 27:5, NLT
2. **He believes in standing for truth** – *"I will maintain my innocence without wavering. My conscience is clear for as long as I live." - Job 27:6, NLT*
3. **His friends keep falsely accusing him** – They assume suffering must mean sin, but Job knows that is not always true.

Job's stance teaches us the importance of **holding firm to truth** even when others misunderstand or wrongly judge us.

Whom Does Job Accuse of Wrongdoing, And Why Is This Problematic?

Job accuses **God** of being responsible for his suffering:

"The Almighty has taken away my rights. In his bitterness, he has made my soul bitter." - Job 27:2, NLT

This is problematic because:

1. **Job does not yet understand the full picture** – He assumes that God is punishing him, when in reality, his suffering is a test.
2. **Job is walking a fine line between lament and accusation** – Though he remains faithful, he struggles with blaming God for his situation.
3. **It challenges the idea of divine justice** – Job questions why the wicked prosper while he, an innocent man, suffers.

This reflects how believers often **wrestle with God in suffering**, struggling to reconcile faith with painful experiences.

Job Saying About "True Wisdom" (Job 28:28)

Job declares that true wisdom is found in fearing the Lord:

"And this is what he says to all humanity: 'The fear of the Lord is true wisdom; to forsake evil is real understanding.'" - Job 28:28, NLT

This means that:

1. Wisdom is not just intellectual knowledge, but reverence for God.
2. True wisdom is moral and spiritual—living rightly before God.
3. Fearing God leads to avoiding evil, which is true understanding.

This echoes **Proverbs 9:10**, which also states: *"The fear of the Lord is the beginning of wisdom."*

Where Do People Today Search For Wisdom Apart From God?

Many people today look for wisdom in **human sources** rather than in God. Some common places include:

1. **Philosophy and human reasoning** – Some seek wisdom in intellectual theories but **reject biblical truth**.
2. **Science and technology** – While valuable, science alone **cannot answer life's deepest questions** about purpose and morality.
3. **Self-help and self-reliance** – Many believe that wisdom comes from **looking within themselves**, ignoring the need for God.
4. **Social media and influencers** – The world often turns to celebrities or social figures for "wisdom" rather than biblical truth.
5. **False religions and mysticism** – Some seek **spiritual enlightenment** through paths that do not align with God's Word.

Job reminds us that the only true wisdom comes from fearing God and living according to His ways.

Conclusion

In **Job 26-29**, Job moves between marveling at **God's greatness**, defending his **own integrity**, and **seeking true wisdom**:

1. God's creation is powerful, yet it is only a whisper of His true greatness.
2. Job maintains his innocence despite false accusations.
3. True wisdom is found in fearing the Lord, not in human knowledge.

This chapter challenges us to trust in God's wisdom over human understanding and to hold firm to integrity even in times of suffering.

CHAPTER 9 - A Life Examined

Job's Suffering, Integrity, and Final Defense

Job Chapter 30 and Chapter 31

Job's suffering makes him a target for ridicule, something he never faced when he was wealthy and respected. Songs and jokes at his expense deepen his humiliation. For the first time, he finds himself on the receiving end of power rather than wielding it, adding to his distress. As he reflects on his conversations with his friends, Job maintains his innocence and sees no justification for their accusations. Believing in God's sovereignty, he holds God responsible for not alleviating his suffering, knowing that God has the power to do so. Eventually, Job reaches a breaking point—he is exhausted by his friends' relentless accusations of hidden sin and frustrated with God's silence. Physically and emotionally overwhelmed, he sees no relief in sight. His experience mirrors that of many who suffer, as despair and hopelessness threaten to consume him in the absence of divine revelation. More than anything, Job longs for God's presence.

In **Job 29**, Job remembers his former days of **honor, prosperity, and God's favor**, but in **Job 30**, he laments how drastically things have changed:

JOB'S PAST BLESSINGS (Job 29)	JOB'S PRESENT SUFFERING (JOB 30)
He was respected & honored- The young and old revered him. (Job 29:7-10)	**He is mocked by outcasts** (Job 30:1) – Even those beneath him in status ridicule him.
He enjoyed God's presence and blessing (Job 29:2-5).	**He feels abandoned by God** (Job 30:20) – "I cry to you, O God, but you don't answer."
He helped the poor, widows, and orphans (Job 29:12-16).	**He is now despised and rejected** (Job 30:10) – "They detest me and keep their distance."
He lived in security and abundance (Job 29:18-20).	**He suffers physically, emotionally, and spiritually** (Job 30:16-19).

Job sees his suffering as **a complete reversal** of his past life, which adds to his confusion—he cannot understand why God would allow such a dramatic fall from grace.

In What Ways Does Job Seek To Show That He Is A Person Of Integrity?

In **Job 31**, Job presents a list of moral commitments that demonstrate his integrity. He essentially takes a **self-imposed oath**, swearing that he has lived righteously in multiple areas of life:

1. **Purity** – *"I made a covenant with my eyes not to look with lust at a young woman." - Job 31:1*
2. **Honesty** – *"If I have walked with falsehood or my foot has rushed to deceit, let God weigh me on the scales of justice." - Job 31:5-6*
3. **Faithfulness in Marriage** – *"If my heart has been seduced by a woman... let my wife belong to another man." - Job 31:9-10*
4. **Justice and Compassion** – *"If I have denied the desires of the poor or let the eyes of the widow grow weary... let my arm fall from the shoulder." - Job 31:16-22*

5. **Avoiding Greed** – *"If I have put my trust in gold or said to pure gold, 'You are my security'..."* - *Job 31:24-25*
6. **Worshiping Only God** – *"If I have rejoiced at my wealth or if I have secretly worshiped the sun or moon..."* - *Job 31:26-28*
7. **Loving his Enemies** – *"If I have rejoiced at my enemy's misfortune or gloated over the trouble that came to him..."* - *Job 31:29-30*

Job is determined to **prove his innocence** by highlighting how he has lived a blameless life, obeying God's moral standards.

These Are All Good Actions, So What Is Job Missing?

While Job's actions are **righteous and commendable**, he is missing **a full understanding of God's sovereignty and grace**:

1. **Job views righteousness to secure blessings** – He believes that because he has lived uprightly, he should not be suffering.

2. **He struggles to accept suffering without explanation** – He cannot understand why God allows the righteous to suffer.
3. **He relies heavily on his own righteousness** – While Job is truly an upright man, he focuses on proving his own moral record instead of fully trusting God's justice.

This reveals an important lesson: *Righteousness is good, but our relationship with God must be based on faith and trust, not just moral behavior.*

How easy is it for you to put your confidence in your good deeds?

It can be easy to fall into the trap of thinking that good behavior should guarantee a trouble-free life. Like Job:

1. We may believe that **if we live righteously, we deserve God's blessings.**
2. We may feel frustrated when **bad things happen despite our faithfulness.**
3. We might compare ourselves to others and **wonder why wicked people seem to prosper.**

However, the story of Job reminds us that **righteousness does not always prevent suffering**—God's ways are higher than our understanding.

Whom Does Job Ask To Answer Him And Bring Out Charges Against Him?

Job pleads for God Himself to answer him, longing for an opportunity to present his case:

> *"Let the Almighty answer me; let my accuser write out the charges against me." - Job 31:35, NLT*

Job is desperate for an explanation. He wants God to either prove his guilt (which he knows is false) or vindicate his innocence.

This sets the stage for God's response in the coming chapters, where God will reveal His wisdom and sovereignty in ways Job never expected.

Conclusion

1. Job's suffering is a stark contrast to his past honor.
2. He presents a strong case for his integrity, listing his moral commitments.

3. However, he still struggles with trusting God's sovereignty beyond his own righteousness.
4. His demand for an answer from God shows his deep longing for justice.

Ultimately, this passage reminds us that while integrity is important, true faith trusts in God's wisdom even when life seems unfair.

CHAPTER 10 - Elihu Speaks

A New Perspective on Suffering and God's Justice

Job Chapter 32 to Job Chapter 34

*After Job and his friends fall silent, **Elihu**, a younger man, speaks. He has waited out of respect, but their failure to refute Job frustrates him. He insists that **true wisdom comes from God**, not age, and offers a new perspective.*

*Elihu rebukes Job for claiming God is silent and unfair. He argues that **God speaks in ways people often miss**—through **dreams, suffering, and mediators**—to correct and refine them. Suffering, he says, is not always punishment but a means of drawing people closer to God.*

*Defending God's justice, Elihu asserts that **God is righteous and impartial**. He sees all actions and repays fairly. No one has the right to challenge Him. Elihu urges Job to submit to God's wisdom rather than accuse Him.*

Though Elihu's perspective differs from Job's friends, he too lacks full understanding, setting the stage for **God's direct response.**

Elihu waits to speak **out of respect for the elders**, believing that wisdom should come with age:

"I am young and you are old, so I held back from telling you what I think. I thought, 'Those who are older should speak, for wisdom comes with age.'" - Job 32:6-7, NLT

However, after hearing Job and his three friends, Elihu becomes **angry** because:

1. Job justifies himself instead of God - Job 32:2
2. Job's friends fail to provide real answers and only condemn him without proving his guilt (Job 32:3

Elihu believes that wisdom comes from God's Spirit, not just age (Job 32:8), so he finally speaks, determined to offer a better perspective.

According to Elihu, what are the ways by which God speaks to people, and how does God use these means to get the attention of people and bring change today?

Elihu argues that God speaks to people in multiple ways:

1. **Through dreams and visions** –
   "For God speaks again and again, though people do not recognize it. He speaks in dreams, in visions of the night." - Job 33:14-15, NLT
   → **Today**, God can still guide people through dreams, though He primarily speaks through His Word.

2. **Through suffering and discipline** –
   "If they listen and obey God, they will be blessed with prosperity throughout their lives. But if they refuse to listen, they will cross over the river of death." - Job 33:19-22, NLT
   → **Today**, suffering can still serve as a wake-up call, leading people to repentance or deeper dependence on God.

3. **Through a mediator or messenger** –
   "But if an angel from heaven appears—a special messenger to intercede for a person and declare that he is upright—God will be gracious and say, 'Rescue him from the grave.'" - Job 33:23-24, NLT

→ **Today**, Jesus Christ is the ultimate mediator between God and humanity (1 Timothy 2:5).

Elihu teaches that God **communicates in many ways to correct, guide, and redeem people**, even when they do not immediately recognize His voice.

Do you think Elihu is right that Job's words dishonor God?

Elihu rebukes Job for speaking as if he is more righteous than God:

"Job speaks without knowledge; his words lack insight." - Job 34:35, NLT

Elihu is partially right—Job, in his pain, does **question God's justice** and **demands an explanation**. However, Job never curses God or abandons faith, so his words come from deep suffering, not rebellion.

This teaches us an important lesson: Even righteous people can struggle with doubt, but honesty before God is not the same as dishonoring Him.

What, According to Elihu, Honors God?

Elihu insists that true honor comes from recognizing God's justice and sovereignty:

1. **God is always just** – *"Listen to me, you who have understanding. Everyone knows that God doesn't sin!" - Job 34:10, NLT*
2. **People must acknowledge their need for Him** – *"If they listen and obey God, they will be blessed." - Job 33:26, NLT*
3. **Repenting when necessary** – *"He makes them listen to correction and commands them to turn from evil." - Job 36:10, NLT*

According to Elihu, honoring God means trusting His justice, listening to His correction, and submitting to His ways.

Conclusion

1. Elihu waits to speak out of respect but finds fault with both Job and his friends.
2. He believes God speaks through dreams, suffering, and mediators to correct and guide people.
3. While Job's words come from pain, Elihu warns that questioning God's justice can dishonor Him.
4. True honor comes from trusting in God's justice and responding to His correction with humility.

This passage challenges us to listen for God's voice, trust in His justice, and remain humble in times of suffering.

CHAPTER 11 - God's Justice and Power

Elihu's Final Declaration

Job Chapter 35 to Job Chapter 37

Elihu continues speaking, challenging Job's belief that righteousness gains no reward (Job 35). He argues that **human actions do not change God**, *but sin and righteousness impact people. Instead of demanding answers, Job should* **trust God rather than complain**.

In Job 36, Elihu emphasizes God's **justice and power**. *He insists that God disciplines the righteous to lead them toward greater blessings. If people listen and turn to Him, they prosper; if they rebel, they suffer.*

In Job 37, Elihu marvels at **God's majesty in creation**, *describing thunderstorms, snow, and powerful winds as signs of His greatness. He reminds Job that* **God's ways are beyond human understanding**, *urging him to humble himself before the Almighty.*

*Elihu's speeches highlight **God's wisdom and sovereignty**, but like Job's other friends, he fails to grasp the deeper purpose of Job's suffering. His words set the stage for* **God's direct response.**

Elihu criticizes Job for making self-centered and incorrect claims about God's justice. He rebukes Job for:

1. **Questioning whether righteousness matters to God**

    "Do you think it is right for you to claim, 'I am righteous before God'?" - Job 35:2, NLT

    - Job has argued that his suffering is undeserved, but Elihu warns that no human can claim perfect righteousness before God.

2. **Implying that sin and righteousness make no difference to God**

    "If you sin, how does that affect God? Even if you sin again and again, what effect will it have on him?" - Job 35:6, NLT

- Elihu rebukes Job for thinking that human actions have no impact on God's justice and righteousness.

3. **Complaining that God does not listen to the cries of the oppressed**

   > *"You say you cannot see him, but he will bring justice if you will only wait." - Job 35:14, NLT*

   - Elihu reminds Job that **God does hear, but He acts in His perfect timing**.

How Do These Claims Reflect People's Attacks On God Even Today?

Many people today question God's justice and fairness, just as Job did:

1. **"If God is good, why do bad things happen to good people?"**
   - Like Job, people struggle to understand why the righteous suffer while the wicked prosper.
2. **"God doesn't care about what I do."**

- Some believe that their actions do not matter to God, much like Job's questioning of whether righteousness makes a difference.

3. **"God doesn't listen to my prayers."**
   - Many, like Job, feel unheard by God during difficult times and assume He is distant or indifferent.

Elihu's response reminds us that God is just, sovereign, and attentive, even when His ways are beyond our understanding.

What aspects of God's character does Elihu bring out that Job may have forgotten?

Elihu emphasizes three key attributes of God that Job may have lost sight of:

1. **God's Justice** – *"God is mighty, but he does not despise anyone! He is mighty in both power and understanding." - Job 36:5, NLT*
   - God is always just, even when His justice is not immediately visible.

2. **God's Power and Sovereignty** – *"Look, God is all-powerful. Who is a teacher like him?" - Job 36:22, NLT*
   - God rules over nature, the weather, and all creation, displaying His control over the universe.
3. **God's Mercy and Discipline** – *"He rescues the poor in their misery and opens their ears in oppression." - Job 36:15, NLT*
   - Elihu points out that suffering can be a means of correction and growth, not just punishment.

Job had been so focused on **his suffering** that he had forgotten the bigger picture of **God's justice, power, and mercy**.

How do Elihu's words regarding God's greatness and mercy cause you to reflect on how you respond to God?

Elihu's speech reminds us to:

1. **Trust in God's justice**, even when life feels unfair
   - Just because we don't see immediate justice doesn't mean God is not working.

2. **Recognize that suffering has a purpose**
   - Like Job, we may not always understand why we suffer, but Elihu reminds us that **God can use trials for discipline, growth, or to draw us closer to Him.**
3. **Remember God's power and greatness**
   - When we focus on our problems, we can forget how great God is. Elihu reminds us that **God is in control, even in storms—both literal and spiritual** (Job 37:13).

Conclusion

1. Elihu corrects Job's mistaken claims about God's justice.
2. He reminds Job that God hears, sees, and acts in His perfect time.
3. He highlights God's justice, power, and mercy, which Job had momentarily forgotten.
4. His words challenge us to trust God's sovereignty, even when we don't understand His ways.

Ultimately, this passage calls us to humility, faith, and a renewed perspective on God's wisdom and justice.

CHAPTER 12 - Where Were You?

God's Challenge and Job's Surrender

Job Chapter 38 to Job 40:5

After a long silence, God finally speaks to Job from a storm (Job 38). Instead of answering Job's questions, God challenges him with a series of questions, revealing His power, wisdom, and control over creation. He asks Job where he was when the earth was formed, who controls the sea, the weather, and the stars. Through these questions, God demonstrates that His ways are beyond human understanding.

In Job 39, God continues by describing the mysteries of the animal kingdom—lions, mountain goats, wild oxen, ostriches, and eagles. Each creature follows God's design, showing His wisdom and sovereignty.

In Job 40:1-2, God directly challenges Job: "Will the one who contends with the Almighty correct Him?" Job is left speechless, realizing his limitations before God's greatness. God's response shifts Job's focus from *demanding answers to humbling himself before divine authority.*

The Lord begins His response out of a whirlwind, directly challenging Job's understanding:

"Who is this that questions my wisdom with such ignorant words? Brace yourself like a man, because I have some questions for you, and you must answer them." - Job 38:2-3, NLT

1. God immediately establishes His authority, making it clear that Job lacks the wisdom to question Him.
2. He does not explain Job's suffering but instead asks a series of questions that reveal His greatness.

God's initial questions are all about the universe and creation. What do these questions reveal to Job?

God asks Job a series of rhetorical questions about creation, such as:

1. "Where were you when I laid the foundations of the earth?" (Job 38:4)
2. "Who kept the sea inside its boundaries?" (Job 38:8)

3. "Can you direct the movement of the stars?" (Job 38:31)

These questions reveal three key truths to Job:

1. **God's wisdom is far beyond human understanding** – Job realizes he has no control over the universe and cannot challenge God's knowledge.
2. **God's power and sovereignty are undeniable** – The world is held together by God's authority, not human reasoning.
3. **Job's place is one of humility** – He is reminded that he is not God and must trust in God's wisdom rather than his own perspective.

Job's First Response to God's Challenge.

After hearing God's powerful questions, Job is humbled and realizes his insignificance:

> *"I am nothing—how could I ever find the answers? I will cover my mouth with my hand. I have said too much already. I have nothing more to say." - Job 40:4-5, NLT*

1. **Job no longer demands an answer** from God; instead, he realizes that God's wisdom is far beyond his comprehension.
2. **He stops speaking**, symbolizing **his surrender to God's authority**.

Job **moves from questioning God to trusting Him**, even without receiving an explanation for his suffering.

What did Job previously ask for that he now receives, and what happens (see Job 13:3)?

Earlier, in **Job 13:3**, Job boldly declared:

"As for me, I would speak directly to the Almighty. I want to argue my case with God himself." - Job 13:3, NLT

Now, in **Job 38:1**, God **finally answers him**—but **not in the way Job expected**:

1. Job wanted a legal argument with God, but instead, God questions him.
2. Job thought he could defend himself, but he realizes he has no defense.

3. Job's confidence turns into humility as he sees the majesty of God.

This teaches that **God may answer our prayers, but not always in the way we expect**—His response often reveals our need for trust rather than explanations.

God's challenge teach us about God and our attitude toward Him.

God's response to Job teaches several important lessons:

1. **God is sovereign and beyond human comprehension** – We cannot fully understand His ways, but we can trust His wisdom.
2. **Humility is the right response to God** – Like Job, we must recognize our limitations and submit to God's authority.
3. **God is not obligated to explain Himself** – Instead of answers, He gives us **His presence and power**, which should be enough.
4. **Faith means trusting even without explanations** – Job's shift from demanding answers to **silently trusting** is an example for all believers.

Conclusion

1. God's response is not an explanation, but a revelation of His power and wisdom.
2. Job's perspective shifts from questioning to humility.
3. We learn that God's ways are higher than ours, and trusting Him is more important than understanding everything.

Ultimately, this passage challenges us to approach God with reverence, trust, and humility, even when life doesn't make sense.

CHAPTER 13 - God's Ultimate Authority and Job's Restoration

Job 40:6 to Job Chapter 42

*God speaks to Job again from the storm (Job 40:6), challenging him to **consider His power**. He asks if Job can judge the world like He does or if he can subdue the proud. To illustrate His unmatched strength, God describes **Behemoth**, a mighty creature beyond human control (Job 40:15-24).*

*In Job 41, God presents **Leviathan**, a terrifying sea creature no one can tame. If no human can overpower such creatures, how much greater is **God's power**? Job, overwhelmed, **admits his insignificance** and repents for questioning God's justice (Job 42:1-6).*

*Finally, God rebukes Job's friends for misrepresenting Him and commands them to offer sacrifices, with Job praying for them (Job 42:7-9). In the end, **God restores Job's fortunes**, blessing him with **twice as much** as before, along with a* *new family and a long life (Job 42:10-17).* **Job's faith is refined, and God's justice prevails.**

In **Job 40:15 – Job 41**, God describes two mighty creatures—**Behemoth and Leviathan**—as symbols of His power and control over creation.

1. **Behemoth (Job 40:15-24)**
    - A massive land creature that is unshakable, powerful, and untamable.

       "Look at Behemoth, which I made along with you… the sinews of its thighs are tightly knit. Its bones are tubes of bronze, its limbs like rods of iron." - Job 40:15-18, NLT

    - **Lesson for Job:** If Job cannot control Behemoth, how could he possibly challenge God?

2. **Leviathan (Job 41:1-34)**
    - A terrifying sea creature, **untouchable by humans and invincible in battle**.

       "Can you catch Leviathan with a hook? Or put a noose around its jaw?" - Job 41:1, NLT

- **Lesson for Job:** If Job cannot subdue Leviathan, how can he demand answers from God?

God's Message To Job

1. **Job is weak compared to God's power** – He cannot control these creatures, let alone the universe.
2. **God's sovereignty is unquestionable** – If He governs such mighty beasts, He certainly governs human affairs.
3. **Job must trust God rather than question His justice** – Just as these creatures are beyond Job's control, so are God's ways.

How Does Job Respond When God Stops Speaking?

After hearing God's challenges, Job humbly surrenders and repents:

> "I know that you can do anything, and no one can stop you. I was talking about things I knew nothing about, things far too wonderful for me." - Job 42:2-3, NLT

1. **Job admits his ignorance** – He realizes he spoke without full knowledge.
2. **He acknowledges God's greatness** – *"I had only heard about you before, but now I have seen you with my own eyes." - Job 42:5, NLT*
3. **He repents in humility** – *"I take back everything I said, and I sit in dust and ashes to show my repentance." - Job 42:6, NLT*

What This Teaches Us

1. True wisdom begins with humility before God.
2. Encountering God's presence changes everything.
3. Instead of demanding answers, faith trusts God's higher purpose.

What does Job's experience teach us about being in God's presence?

Job's encounter with God teaches that:

1. **God's presence brings perspective** – When Job sees God's majesty, his personal suffering seems small.

2. **Being before God leads to humility** – Instead of justifying himself, Job repents and acknowledges his limitations.
3. **We don't always get explanations, but we receive revelation** – God never tells Job why he suffered, but Job sees God more clearly, which is enough.
4. **God's presence transforms us** – Job moves from demanding justice to trusting God completely.

This reminds us that when we seek God, we don't always get answers, but we get Him—and that is enough.

Why Does The Lord Require Job To Pray For His Friends, And How Does The Lord Bless Job After He Prays?

God rebukes Job's friends for their wrong assumptions about Him:

"I am angry with you and your two friends because you have not spoken the truth about me, as my servant Job has." - Job 42:7, NLT

Why Must Job Pray for Them?

1. Job's friends misrepresented God, so their forgiveness required intercession.
2. God calls Job to act in mercy, despite their attacks.
3. This act restores both Job and his friends before God.

Job's Blessing After He Prays

"When Job prayed for his friends, the Lord restored his fortunes. In fact, the Lord gave him twice as much as before!" - Job 42:10, NLT

1. **Job's obedience leads to restoration** – He receives **double what he lost**.
2. **He is honored again in his community** – *"All his brothers, sisters, and former friends came and feasted with him." - Job 42:11, NLT*
3. **God gives him a long, full life** – *"Job lived 140 years, seeing four generations." - Job 42:16, NLT*

This shows that blessing follows obedience and humility before God.

Why would God call on Job to intercede for those who had attacked him?

God asks Job to pray for his friends **as an act of mercy and forgiveness**.

1. **It teaches Job to extend grace** – Just as Job received mercy from God, he must now extend it to his friends.
2. **It corrects the friends' false theology** – They assumed suffering = sin, but now they must learn humility.
3. **It restores relationships** – Job and his friends are reconciled before God and one another.
4. **It demonstrates God's justice and mercy** – **Forgiveness is an essential part of God's plan**.

Lesson for Us

1. **Forgiveness is powerful** – Job's prayer was required before full restoration came.
2. **God honors those who extend mercy** – Even when wronged, we are called to **intercede for others**.

3. **Healing often comes through acts of obedience** – Job's final blessing came **after** he prayed for his friends.

Conclusion

1. God uses Behemoth and Leviathan to humble Job, showing His power over all creation.
2. Job responds with humility, repentance, and trust in God.
3. God restores Job, but only after he prays for his friends, teaching the importance of mercy.
4. True faith is not about getting answers, but about trusting God's sovereignty and forgiving others.

Job's story teaches us that God is always just, always powerful, and always faithful—even when we don't understand His ways.

CHAPTER 14 – Lessons From Job's Story

The Book of Job ultimately teaches that **faith is not merely about receiving blessings but about trusting God even in the silence**. Job never received an explanation for his suffering, but he encountered God in a profound way. His story reminds us that God's wisdom surpasses human reasoning, and His plans are always purposeful, even when they seem hidden.

1. Faithfulness in Suffering

- Job was a righteous man, yet he suffered greatly. This teaches us that suffering is not always a result of sin but can be a test of faith.
- Even when Job lost everything—his wealth, family, and health—he remained faithful to God, saying, **"The Lord gave and the Lord has taken away; blessed be the name of the Lord"** - Job 1:21

2. God's Sovereignty Over Everything

- Job's suffering was permitted by God but caused by Satan. This shows that **nothing happens without God's knowledge and permission**.
- Sometimes, we may not understand why we suffer, but God has a greater purpose beyond what we can see.

3. Trusting God Even Without Answers

- Job questioned God, but God did not give him direct answers. Instead, God reminded Job of His power and wisdom (Job 38–41).
- This teaches us to **trust God even when we don't understand His ways** (Isaiah 55:8-9).

4. True Friends Offer Comfort, Not Judgment

- Job's friends (Eliphaz, Bildad, and Zophar) wrongly assumed that he was suffering because of sin.
- This teaches us that when people are suffering, **we should offer compassion, not judgment** (Galatians 6:2).

5. God Can Restore What Was Lost

- In the end, God **restored Job's fortunes** and blessed him with even more than he had before (Job 42:10-17).
- This shows that **God is a redeemer who can turn our suffering into blessings**.

6. Humility Before God

- Job learned to humble himself before God and recognize His greatness (Job 42:1-6).
- When we face trials, we should acknowledge that **God is in control and submit to His will**.

7. God Rewards Perseverance

- Job endured suffering and was ultimately rewarded. This aligns with **James 5:11** :

  "As you know, we count as blessed those who have persevered. You have heard of Job's perseverance and have seen what the Lord finally brought about. The Lord is full of compassion and mercy."

Conclusion:

The story of Job teaches us to

1. Trust God in difficult times,
2. Remain faithful despite suffering,
3. Believe that God's plans are always for our good (Romans 8:28).
4. Even when life feels unfair, God is still in control, and
5. He will bring restoration in His perfect time.

Epilogue

Suffering is one of life's greatest mysteries—an experience that humble even the strongest of believers. The story of Job reveals that pain does not always come because of sin, nor does it mean that God has abandoned us. Instead, suffering refines us, deepens our faith, and draws us closer to the wisdom and sovereignty of our Creator.

Through Job's journey, we learn that even when God is silent, He is not absent. His plans unfold in ways we may not understand, but His love remains steadfast. Job never received all the answers he sought, but in the end, he encountered God in a profound way, realizing that **God's wisdom far surpasses human understanding.**

Likewise, in our own trials, we may not always get explanations, but we can rest in the assurance that **our Redeemer lives**, and He is faithful to restore, heal, and fulfill His greater purpose in our lives.

May this book serve as a reminder that silence is not the absence of God—it is often the space where He does His deepest work in us.

To Him be the glory, now and forever. Amen.

Acknowledgments

First and foremost, I give **all glory and honor to God**, whose guidance and presence sustain me through every step of this journey. Even in times of silence, His faithfulness never fails.

Writing this book has been a journey of faith, reflection, and deep reliance on God's wisdom. I am grateful to all those who have played a part in bringing this work to life.

To my **family**, especially my beloved wife, Amy—thank you for your love, prayers, and unwavering support. Your encouragement has been my strength in moments of doubt. To my children and grandchildren, you are my greatest blessings and inspiration.

To my **church family at City of Grace Christian Church**, my fellow pastors, and the brothers and sisters in Christ who have encouraged me in my ministry—thank you for your prayers, support, and shared faith.

To those who have endured suffering yet remained faithful—your stories have inspired me to write this book.

May it bring comfort and renewed faith to all who seek answers in life's trials.

Finally, to **my readers**, thank you for taking this journey through the life of Job with me. May you find hope, strength, and assurance that even when God seems silent, He is always working for your good.

About the Author

W. A. Almilla, also known as **Kuyawill**, is a passionate minister of the Gospel, a dedicated teacher of biblical truth. He has spent years serving in ministry, witnessing firsthand the struggles, faith, and perseverance of those enduring life's most difficult trials.

Originally from the Philippines, he moved to the United States in 1999 and has since been actively involved in Christian ministry. He currently serves as one of the pastors at **City of Grace Christian Church in Las Vegas, Nevada**, where he continues to preach, teach, and encourage others in their walk with Christ.

His writing focuses on exploring the depths of Scripture, providing insight into God's wisdom, and helping believers strengthen their faith. His previous works include *Matthew Unveiled: A Comprehensive Study Guide*, *A Journey Through Parables*, and *The Seeds of Purpose: A Journey Through the Soil of Life*.

In ***When God Seems Silent: Lessons from Job***, he seeks to address one of the most challenging aspects of faith—

trusting God amid suffering. Through the story of Job, he offers encouragement to those who find themselves in seasons of silence, reminding them that God's purpose is greater than their pain.

Printed in Great Britain
by Amazon

1e472670-61aa-41ee-b358-f69d4d0f7ffeR01